THE TRUTH ABOUT

ARMAGEDDON AND THE MIDDLE EAST

THOMAS ICE AND TIMOTHY DEMY

HARVEST HOUSE PUBLISHERS
Eugene, Oregon 97402

Scripture quotations are taken from the New American Standard Bible, © 1960, 1962, 1963, 1968, 1971, 1972, 1973, 1975, 1977 by The Lockman Foundation. Used by permission.

Cover design by Left Coast Design, Portland, Oregon.

**THE TRUTH ABOUT ARMAGEDDON
AND THE MIDDLE EAST**

Copyright © 1997 by Pre-Trib Research Center
Published by Harvest House Publishers
Eugene, Oregon 97402

ISBN 1–56507–683-4

Printed in the United States of America.

97 98 99 00 01 02 / LP / 10 9 8 7 6 5 4 3 2 1

Contents

————————— **PART 3** —————————

What Else Do We Know About Armageddon?

————————— **PART 4** —————————

Why Does Armageddon Matter?

About this series...

The Pocket Prophecy Series is designed to provide readers with a brief summary of individual topics and issues in Bible prophecy. For quick reference and ease in studying, the works are written in a question-and-answer format. The questions follow a logical progression so that people who read straight through will receive a greater appreciation for the topic and the issues involved. Each issue is fully documented and contains a bibliography of recommended reading for those people who desire to pursue their study in greater depth.

The theological perspective presented throughout the series is that of premillennialism and pretribulationism. We recognize that this is not the only position embraced by evangelical Christians, but we believe that it is the most widely held and prominent perspective. It is also our conviction that premillennialism and, specifically, pretribulationism, best explains the prophetic plan of God as revealed in the Bible.

The study of prophecy and its puzzling pieces is an endeavor that is detailed and complex—but not beyond comprehension or resolution. It is open to error, misinterpretation, and confusion. Such possibilities should not, however, cause any Christian to shy away from either the study of prophecy or engagement in honest and helpful discussions about it. The goal of this series is to provide all those who desire to better understand the Scriptures with a concise and consistent tool. If you will do the digging, the rewards will be great and the satisfaction will remain with you as you grow in your knowledge and love of our Lord Jesus Christ and His Word.

INTRODUCTION

Throughout history countless battles, campaigns, and wars have been waged across the earth. Some have been limited in scope; others have been global. Armies have fought because of land and leaders, love and loyalty, for causes that have been just and, more often, unjust. The pain, suffering, and death inflicted from these conflicts and ones in our own day are beyond measure.

The Bible tells us that the future will also be filled with war. There is one major prophetic conflict that has captured the attention of Christians and non-Christians throughout the centuries—Armageddon. This event is prophesied to be the most catastrophic and devastating occurrence in human history. Whether or not people believe it will really happen, they readily identify with the magnitude of its symbolism. It is directly and indirectly spoken of in literature, movies, propaganda, political debates, sermons, and cultural commentaries. Everyone, it seems, has some notion or vague idea about it. Some of the ideas are biblical; many are not.

There is only one place to find accurate information about Armageddon—the Bible. In its prophetic pages we read not only of Armageddon, but of the events that precede and follow this final war of world history. Although we aren't given all the details of Armageddon, we are provided with an overall glimpse of God's plans for the future.

Why does the Bible speak of Armageddon? Because it affirms God's sovereignty over history and reminds us that there is a divine purpose and plan that will not be thwarted. God will one day right all wrongs, judge all evil, and establish a universal reign of righteousness. The hope of Christians throughout the centuries will be realized with the second coming of Jesus Christ and the defeat of those who oppose Him at Armageddon. It is because of this hope that we study prophecy, waiting for the fulfillment of God's promises.

PART 1

What Does the Bible Say About Armageddon?

1. Where does the Bible teach about the conflict of Armageddon?

We read of Armageddon in Daniel 11:40-45; Joel 3:9-17; Zechariah 14:1-3; and Revelation 16:14-16. This great battle will occur in the final days of the tribulation. John tells us that the kings of the world will be gathered together "for the war of the great day of

God, the almighty" in a place known as Har-Magedon (Revelation 16:14,16). The site for the converging of the armies is the plain of Esdraelon, around the hill of Megiddo. This area is located in northern Israel about 20 miles south-southeast of Haifa.

According to the Bible, great armies from the east and the west will gather on this plain. The Antichrist will respond to threats to his power from the south. He will also move to destroy a revived Babylon in the east before finally turning his forces toward Jerusalem. (For hundreds of years Babylon, located in present-day Iran, was one of the world's most important cities. According to Revelation 14:8; 16:9; and 17–18, it will again arise in the last days as a powerful religious, social, political, and economical city.) As the Antichrist and his armies move on Jerusalem, God will intervene and Jesus Christ will return. The Lord will destroy the armies, capture the Antichrist and the False Prophet, and cast them into the lake of fire (Revelation 19:11-21).

When the Lord returns, the power and rule of the Antichrist will come to an end. Dr. Charles Dyer writes of this event:

> Daniel, Joel, and Zechariah identify Jerusalem as the site where the final battle between Antichrist and Christ will occur. All three predict that God will intervene in history on behalf of His people and will destroy the Antichrist's army at Jerusalem. Zechariah predicts that the battle will end when the Messiah returns to earth and His feet touch down on the Mount of Olives. This battle concludes with the second coming of Jesus to earth. . . . The battle is over before it even begins.[1]

The battle of Armageddon—actually at Jerusalem—will be the most anticlimactic combat in history. As John describes the armies mustered on both sides, we expect to witness some epic struggle between good and evil. Yet no matter how mighty someone on earth is, that individual is no match for the power of God.

2. Will the conflict of Armageddon be a real battle?

Armageddon prophecy is not literary allegory or myth. Armageddon will be a real event of tragic proportions for those who oppose God. It will be a converging of actual military forces in the Middle East on some of the most contested land of all time—a land that has never known lasting peace. It is also a spiritual battle between the forces of good and evil. It will conclude with divine intervention and the return of Jesus Christ.

3. Where will Armageddon take place?

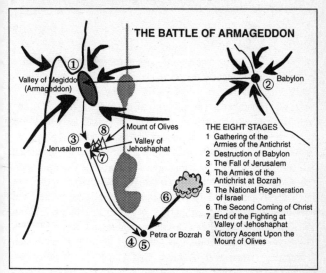

THE BATTLE OF ARMAGEDDON

Valley of Megiddo (Armageddon)

Babylon

Mount of Olives

③ Jerusalem

⑧

Valley of Jehoshaphat

⑦

⑥

④⑤ Petra or Bozrah

THE EIGHT STAGES

1 Gathering of the Armies of the Antichrist
2 Destruction of Babylon
3 The Fall of Jerusalem
4 The Armies of the Antichrist at Bozrah
5 The National Regeneration of Israel
6 The Second Coming of Christ
7 End of the Fighting at Valley of Jehoshaphat
8 Victory Ascent Upon the Mount of Olives

As noted earlier, the armies will converge on the plain of Esdraelon, around the hill of Megiddo. John writes in Revelation 16:16, "And they gathered them together to the place which in Hebrew is called Har-Magedon." This area is located in northern Israel about 20 miles south-southeast of Haifa and 50 miles north of Jerusalem. The area was the scene of many battles in Old Testament times. For instance, Judges 4 records it as the area of Barak's conflict with the Canaanites, and it was also the area of Gideon's battle with the Midianites recorded in Judges 7.

However, Armageddon is not the site of the final battle or of the actual fighting. It is, rather, a place where the forces will assemble as they prepare for this tumultuous and terrible conflict. It is a staging area where final preparations are made. Dr. Arnold Fruchtenbaum writes:

> It should be noted that the passage [Revelation 16:12-16] says nothing of a battle in this valley for no fighting will take place here. The Valley of Jezreel, guarded by the mountain of Megiddo, will merely serve as the gathering ground for the armies of the Antichrist. Armageddon will play the same role that England played in the closing conflicts of World War II. The allied forces gathered their armies together in England but that is not where the final battle took place. The final battle began on the beaches of Normandy, France, on "D" Day. Armageddon will also serve as the gathering place with the battle beginning elsewhere.[3]

4. How do we know Armageddon won't happen today or tomorrow?

God has a detailed plan. Many prophetic events have already been fulfilled, including the birth, death, and resurrection of Jesus Christ 2,000 years ago. Many other events, such as the rapture of the church, the seven-year tribulation, the second coming of Christ, and the millennial kingdom are yet to come. The prophecies related to these events will be fulfilled as certainly as were the events of the past. However, they will also be brought to fruition in accordance with God's specific timing. There is a chronology and sequence to His plan.

According to God's plan there are several major events which will transpire before the campaign of Armageddon commences. The next major event is the rapture of the church spoken of in 1 Thessalonians 4:13-18 and elsewhere.[4] Conflicts, battles, and wars around the globe are part of our daily headlines. Lasting peace in the Middle East is a commendable and desirable goal, but, according to the Bible, it is a dream that will not be attained in our day. There will be more conflicts in the Middle East and around the world, but these are not to be associated with Armageddon because some prophesied events precede this battle. Armageddon won't happen in the near future because at least seven years of tribulation must precede it.

5. When will the conflict of Armageddon occur?

Though there is often mention of the conflict of Armageddon in today's popular culture, it will not take place tomorrow, next month, or next year. We believe that it is a military conflict that occurs *after* the rapture and at the end of the seven-year tribulation. However, not all premillennial and pretribulational interpreters place it at the end of the tribulation.[5] It is our understanding that it will be the culmination of the Antichrist's reign, and it will end with the second coming of Jesus Christ and the destruction of the Antichrist and his forces.

Armageddon is the last major event on the prophetic timeline before the establishment of the millennial kingdom, Christ's 1,000-year reign on earth. Armageddon is not an event that people should desire or anticipate with joy because it will bring death and destruction. It is, however, a definite future military conflict that will not, and cannot, be avoided by any amount of negotiation.

6. Is Armageddon a single battle or a campaign?

The detailed sequence of events and the terms used in relation to Armageddon suggest that it will be a campaign or series of battles. While it is not inappropriate to speak of it as the "final battle," or to use other similar language, technically we should probably refer to it as a campaign or the war of Armageddon. The Greek word *polemos,* translated "war" in Revelation 16:14, usually signifies an extended war or campaign. A single battle or fight is normally referred to by the word *mache.* An example of a passage where both terms are used is found in James 4:1, where James writes of interpersonal conflict: "What is the source of quarrels *[polemos]* and conflicts *[mache]* among you? Is not the source your pleasures that wage war *[strateuomai]* in your members?"

Armageddon is not a single battle, and the battles do not occur in a single day. One of the last phases of Armageddon is three days in duration. The battles are carried out over a wide geographic area to the north and south of Jerusalem and as far east as Babylon.

PART 2

What Is the Course of the Campaign?

7. What is the sequence and content of the stages of Armageddon?

Although the sequence of events is not found in one specific verse, detailed study of all the biblical passages pertaining to Armageddon reveals a very complex campaign. One of the most thorough studies of the campaign is that of Dr. Arnold Fruchtenbaum, who has divided the campaign into eight stages.[6] Although other plans can just as readily be proposed, his evaluation seems to be the most logical and comprehensive. Dr. Fruchtenbaum writes:

> The two climactic events of the Great Tribulation are the Campaign of Armageddon and the second coming of Jesus Christ. A considerable amount of data is given about this time period in the Scriptures. One of the greatest difficulties in the study of eschatology is placing these events in chronological sequence in order to see what exactly will happen in the Campaign of Armageddon. . . . The Campaign of Armageddon can be divided into eight stages, and this in turn will facilitate an understanding of the sequence of events.[7]

Each of these eight stages serves a distinct purpose in the overall campaign. Each stage builds in anticipation and intensity until the climax at the second coming of Christ.

Stage 1: The Antichrist's Allies Assemble

The primary biblical reference to this first stage is Revelation 16:12-16:

> And the sixth angel poured out his bowl upon the great river, the Euphrates; and its water was dried up, that the way might be prepared for the kings from the east. And I saw coming out of the mouth of the dragon and out of the mouth of the beast and out of the mouth of the false prophet, three unclean spirits like frogs; for they are spirits of demons, performing signs, which go out to the kings of the whole world, to gather them together for the war of the great day of God, the Almighty. ("Behold, I am coming like a thief. Blessed is the one who stays awake and keeps his garments, lest he walk about naked and men see his shame.") And they gathered them together to the place which in Hebrew is called Har-Magedon.

The assembling of the armies begins at the same time as the divine judgment of the sixth bowl. At this time the Euphrates River will be dried up, making it faster and easier for the armies of the "kings from the east" to assemble. In the Bible, "east" refers to the region of Mesopotamia (Assyria and Babylon), and the drying up of the river will make it easier for the forces of the Antichrist to assemble out of Babylon, which is his capital. The armies joining him will be those of the seven remaining kings out of the ten described in Daniel 7:24-27 and Revelation 17:12,13. Their goal will be the final destruction of the Jews.

Writing of the satanic and demonic powers behind this coalition, Dr. Fruchtenbaum states:

> The gathering for this final campaign against the Jews is clearly the work of the counterfeit trinity. All three members of the counterfeit trinity are involved: the dragon, or Satan who is the counterfeit father; the Prophet who is the counterfeit son; and the False Prophet who is the counterfeit holy spirit. The summons will be reenforced by demonic activity to make sure that the nations will indeed cooperate in assembling their armies together. These demonic messengers will be empowered to perform signs in order to assure compliance and defeat any reluctance to fall into line on the part of the other kings.[8]

Stage 2: Babylon Destroyed

In this stage, the activity shifts from the gathering armies of the Antichrist to the destruction of Babylon. While the Antichrist is with his armies at Armageddon, his capital will be attacked and destroyed. In the Old Testament, Babylon was both the place of

Israel's captivity and the originating site of idolatry. Known also as Shinar (Genesis 10:10; 11:2; Daniel 1:2; Zechariah 5:11), Babylon will be a worldwide economic and religious center of activity during the tribulation (Revelation 17–18).

Two of the key passages regarding Babylon's future destruction are found in Jeremiah 50–51 and Revelation 18 (see also Isaiah 13–14). In these chapters we read of a future destruction of the city and nation, one that looks far beyond its first destruction in 539 B.C. In Jeremiah 50:1-10, divine judgment is pronounced against Babylon, and then in verses 11-16, the fall of Babylon is pictured. The warfare will be intense and the destruction will be massive. We read in these verses:

> Because you are glad, because you are jubilant, O you who pillage My heritage, because you skip about like a threshing heifer and neigh like stallions, your mother will be greatly ashamed, she who gave you birth will be humiliated. Behold, she will be the least of the nations, a wilderness, a parched land, and a desert. Because of the indignation of the LORD she will not be inhabited, but she will be completely desolate; everyone who passes by Babylon will be horrified and will hiss because of all her wounds. Draw up your battle lines against Babylon on every side, all you who bend the bow; shoot at her, do not be sparing with your arrows, for she has sinned against the LORD. Raise your battle cry against her on every side! She has given herself up, her pillars have fallen, her walls have been torn down. For this is the vengeance of the LORD: take vengeance on her; as she has done to others, so do to her. Cut off the sower from Babylon, and the one who wields the sickle at the time of harvest; from before the sword of the oppressor they will each turn back to his own people, and they will each flee to his own land (Jeremiah 50:11-16).

A few verses later the description of the destruction continues:

> "Against the land of Merathaim, go up against it, and against the inhabitants of Pekod. Slay and utterly destroy them," declares the LORD, "and do according to all that I have commanded you. The noise of battle is in the land, and great destruction. How the hammer of the whole earth has been cut off and broken! How Babylon has become an object of horror among the nations! I set a snare for you, and you were also caught, O Babylon, while you yourself were not aware; you have been found and also seized because you have engaged in conflict with the LORD. The LORD has opened His armory and has brought forth the weapons of His indignation,

for it is a work of the Lord GOD of hosts in the land of the Chaldeans. Come to her from the farthest border; open up her barns, Pile her up like heaps and utterly destroy her, let nothing be left to her. Put all her young bulls to the sword; let them go down to the slaughter! Woe be upon them, for their day has come, the time of their punishment" (Jeremiah 50:20-27).

According to Isaiah 13:19 and Jeremiah 50:40, the destruction will be as devastating and complete as was that of Sodom and Gomorrah. Once the attack and destruction are finished, Babylon will be uninhabitable and will never again be rebuilt (Revelation 18:21-24).

Who will come against the Antichrist, and what forces will contest his authority and power? According to Jeremiah 50:9 and 50:41,42, the attackers will be an alliance of forces from north of Babylon.

For behold, I am going to arouse and bring up against Babylon a horde of great nations from the land of the north, and they will draw up their battle lines against her; from there she will be taken captive. Their arrows will be like an expert warrior who does not return empty-handed (Jeremiah 50:9).

Behold, a people is coming from the north, and a great nation and many kings will be aroused from the remote parts of the earth. They seize their bow and javelin; they are cruel and have no mercy. Their voice roars like the sea, and they ride on horses, marshalled like a man for the battle against you, O daughter of Babylon (Jeremiah 50:41,42).

Although the Antichrist will be a world ruler, his control will not be so absolute as to preclude rebellion or opposition (Daniel 11:41). He will try, but it will be tactically impossible. The destruction will come as divine punishment for Babylon's long history of antagonism and evil against the people of Israel, and the result will be the razing of the city. "Because Babylon has ruled the entire world ruinously, God will now destroy her that had destroyed so many."[9]

"But I will repay Babylon and all the inhabitants of Chaldea for all their evil that they have done in Zion before your eyes," declares the LORD. "Behold, I am against you, O destroying mountain, who destroys the whole earth," declares the LORD, "and I will stretch out My hand against you, and roll you down from the crags and I will make you a burnt out mountain. And they will not take from you even a stone for a corner nor a stone for foundations, but you will be desolate forever," declares the LORD (Jeremiah 51:24,25).

Although Babylon will be destroyed, the victors will not necessarily know that they are acting on behalf of God and fulfilling His prophetic plan. Their motives will be personal and political rather than prophetic. When Babylon is destroyed, the Antichrist will not be present in the city. He will be told of its destruction by messengers (Jeremiah 50:43; 51:31,32).

The attack will be swift, but there will be some warning or opportunity for Jews who are living in Babylon to flee from the city (Jeremiah 50:6-8,28; 51:5,6). Even in these last days, God will preserve a remnant of His people. These refugees are to go to Jerusalem and tell them of the city's destruction and their escape (Jeremiah 51:10,45,50; Revelation 18:4,5).

The destruction of Babylon will occur at the same time the nation of Israel begins to turn to God for spiritual renewal and regeneration (Jeremiah 31:31-34; 50:19,20). According to Revelation 18:1-3, after Babylon's destruction it will become a place of demonic habitation. Because of its political and economic prominence there will be great confusion, chaos, and despair over Babylon's destruction. The leaders and rulers who aligned themselves with the Antichrist, the merchants and those who prospered because of Babylon, and those who transported and moved commercial goods throughout the world will all be greatly affected by Babylon's fall and will lament their losses (Revelation 18:9-18).

Stage 3: Jerusalem Falls

Although the Antichrist's capital will have been destroyed in the second phase of the campaigning, his forces will not have been lost. Rather than moving eastward to confront the attackers of his capital, the Antichirst will move south against Jerusalem. We read of this move in Zechariah 12:1-3 and 14:1,2:

> The burden of the word of the LORD concerning Israel. Thus declares the LORD who stretches out the heavens, lays the foundation of the earth, and forms the spirit of man within him, "Behold, I am going to make Jerusalem a cup that causes reeling to all the peoples around; and when the siege is against Jerusalem, it will also be against Judah. And it will come about in that day that I will make Jerusalem a heavy stone for all the peoples; all who lift it will be severely injured. And all the nations of the earth will be gathered against it."

Behold, a day is coming for the LORD when the spoil taken from you will be divided among you. For I will gather all the nations against Jerusalem to battle, and the city will be captured, the houses plundered, the women ravished, and half of the city exiled, but the rest of the people will not be cut off from the city.

The Antichrist's forces will sweep down to Jerusalem, and once again the city will fall into Gentile control. Although there will be a temporary resurgence of Jewish strength and stiff resistance, as described in Zechariah 12:4-9 and Micah 4:11–5:1, Jerusalem will fall. The losses on both sides will be enormous, but the Antichrist's forces will prevail initially. However, these passages teach the eventual victory of Israel through the Messiah.

Stage 4: The Antichrist Moves South Against the Remnant

In the fourth stage, the campaign shifts into the desert and mountains, probably to a location about 80 miles south of Jerusalem to the area of Bozrah/Petra. At the beginning of the second half of the tribulation, after the Antichrist breaks his treaty with Israel (Daniel 9:27; Matthew 24:15), many of the Jews will flee into the desert for safety. This activity will be a fulfillment of the words and exhortations of Jesus in Matthew 24:16-31. In verse 16 Jesus says of those who see the abomination of desolation: "Then let those who are in Judea flee to the mountains." This flight for life is also described in Revelation 12:6,14.

After Jerusalem is captured, the Antichrist will move south in an attempt to destroy those who fled in the previous three-and-a-half years. In Micah 2:12 we read of God's gathering and protection of this remnant: "I will surely assemble all of you, Jacob, I will surely gather the remnant of Israel. I will put them together like sheep in the fold; like a flock in the midst of its pasture they will be noisy with men." The area normally associated with this part of the campaign is that of Mount Seir, about 30 miles south of the lower end of the Dead Sea. Two specific sites in that area are possibilities for the location of the fleeing Jews: Bozrah and Petra.[10] In Isaiah 33:13-16 we read of the gathering of the Jews in this area during the last half of the tribulation. In Jeremiah 49:13,14 we read of the gathering of the armies in Bozrah to destroy them. As the Antichrist's forces gather in the rugged wilderness, the fourth phase will come to an end, and the last few days of the campaign will begin.

Stage 5: The Regeneration of Israel

The campaign of Armageddon will culminate in the second coming of Christ. But before Christ returns there will be a confession of

Israel's national sin (Leviticus 26:40-42; Deuteronomy 4:29-31; 30:6-8; Jeremiah 3:11-18; Hosea 5:15), and a pleading for the Messiah to return (Isaiah 64; Zechariah 12:10; Matthew 23:37-39). This will come as the armies of the Antichrist are gathered to destroy the Jews in the wilderness. According to Hosea 6:1-3, there will be a call issued by the Jewish leaders for the nation to repent. The nation will respond positively and repentance will take place for two days. Dr. Fruchtenbaum writes:

> The leaders of Israel will finally recognize the reason why the tribulation has fallen on them. Whether this will be done by the study of the Scriptures, or by the preaching of the 144,000, or via the Two Witnesses (the third sign of Jonah to which the Jews of Jerusalem had already responded), or by the ministry of Elijah, is not clearly stated. Most likely there will be a combination of these things. But the leaders will come to a realization of the national sin in some way. Just as the Jewish leaders once led the nation to the rejection of the Messiahship of Jesus, they will then lead the nation to the acceptance of His Messiahship by issuing the call of Hosea 6:1-3. The confession of Israel's national sin will last for two days as the entire nation becomes regenerated and saved.[11]

The people of Israel will confess their sins with the words of Isaiah 53:1-9 and will be saved, fulfilling the prophecy of Romans 11:25-27:

> For I do not want you, brethren, to be uninformed of this mystery, lest you be wise in your own estimation, that a partial hardening has happened to Israel until the fulness of the Gentiles has come in; and thus all Israel will be saved; just as it is written, "The Deliverer will come from Zion, He will remove ungodliness from Jacob. And this is My covenant with them, when I take away their sins."

The pleading for the return of the Messiah will be done by the Jews in the wilderness as well as those in Jerusalem, and, thus, the prophecy of Joel 2:28-32 will be fulfilled. At this same time, Zechariah 13:2-6 states that false prophets who have arisen during the tribulation and led Israel astray will be executed. Tragically, according to Zechariah 13:7-9, two-thirds of the Jewish population will have been killed during the tribulation. The remaining one-third will confess their sins, and God will answer their pleading for the return of the Messiah. This pleading is spoken of in Isaiah 64:1-12 as well as Psalms 79 and 80. "Only by faith in the Son of Man can Israel be regenerated. Only by calling upon the name of the Lord can Israel be saved spiritually. Only by the return of the Son of Man can Israel be saved physically."[12]

The fifth stage will come to completion on the third day of Israel's confession and prayer for Messiah's return. In the sixth stage, God will answer them, fulfilling biblical prophecy and the hope of the ages.

Stage 6: The Second Coming of Jesus Christ

In the sixth stage the prayers of the Jews are answered. Jesus Christ will return to earth to defeat the armies of the Antichrist at Bozrah and begin the final portions of the campaign. He will return to earth in the clouds, in the same manner in which He departed (Matthew 24:30; Acts 1:9-11). The fact the Jesus returns first to the mountain wilderness of Bozrah is seen from Isaiah 34:1-7; 63:1-6; Habakkuk 3:3; and Micah 2:12,13. At His second coming Jesus Christ, the Messiah, will enter battle with the Antichrist's forces, and fighting without human assistance, with the word of His mouth. He will miraculously defeat them.

According to Jude 14–15 and Revelation 19:11-16, Jesus will return with an angelic army and with the church saints who had been raptured prior to the tribulation. From the verses in Revelation, it is clear that the second coming will bring destruction to the enemies of Jesus Christ:

> And I saw heaven opened; and behold, a white horse, and He who sat upon it is called Faithful and True; and in righteousness He judges and wages war. And His eyes are a flame of fire, and upon His head are many diadems; and He has a name written upon Him which no one knows except Himself. And He is clothed with a robe dipped in blood; and His name is called The Word of God. And the armies which are in heaven, clothed in fine linen, white and clean, were following Him on white horses. And from His mouth comes a sharp sword, so that with it He may smite the nations; and He will rule them with a rod of iron; and He treads the wine press of the fierce wrath of God, the Almighty. And on His robe and on His thigh He has a name written, "KING OF KINGS, AND LORD OF LORDS."

Stage 7: The Final Battle

In the seventh phase, Jesus the Messiah will fight alone on Israel's behalf, destroying the Antichrist and those who have come against the nation and persecuted it. In this phase the Antichrist will be slayed by the true Christ (Habakkuk 3:13; 2 Thessalonians 2:8). "Among the very first casualties will be the Antichrist himself.

Having ruled the world with great power and spoken against the true Son of God, the counterfeit son will be powerless before Christ."[13]

Beginning at Bozrah and moving back to Jerusalem and the Kidron Valley (also known as the Valley of Jehoshaphat), Jesus, the Messiah and King of the Jews, will miraculously engage and destroy the Antichrist's forces (Joel 3:12,13; Zechariah 14:12-15; Revelation 14:19,20).

Stage 8: The Ascent to the Mount of Olives

With the destruction of the Antichrist and his forces complete, the campaign will be over and Jesus will go and stand on the Mount of Olives in a symbolic victory ascent. When He does so, there will be a number of cataclysmic events that will bring the tribulation to an end. As described in Zechariah and Revelation:

> Then the LORD will go forth and fight against those nations, as when He fights on a day of battle. And in that day His feet will stand on the Mount of Olives, which is in front of Jerusalem on the east; and the Mount of Olives will be split in its middle from east to west by a very large valley, so that half of the mountain will move toward the north and the other half toward the south (Zechariah 14:3,4).

> And the seventh angel poured out his bowl upon the air; and a loud voice came out of the temple from the throne, saying, "It is done." And there were flashes of lightning and sounds and peals of thunder; and there was a great earthquake, such as there had not been since man came to be upon the earth, so great an earthquake was it, and so mighty. And the great city was split into three parts, and the cities of the nations fell. And Babylon the great was remembered before God, to give her the cup of the wine of His fierce wrath. And every island fled away, and the mountains were not found. And huge hailstones, about one hundred pounds each, came down from heaven upon men; and men blasphemed God because of the plague of the hail, because its plague was extremely severe (Revelation 16:17-21).

The supernatural calamities that come upon the world at this time, including the greatest earthquake the world has known, correspond to the seventh bowl judgment. As a result of the earthquake, Jerusalem will split into three areas and the Mount of Olives will split into two parts, creating a valley. This is the means of escape from the earthquake for the Jewish inhabitants of the city (Zechariah 14:4,5).

In addition to the earthquake there will be a tremendous hail-storm and a blackout with an eclipse or darkening of the sun and moon (Joel 3:14-16; Matthew 24:29). With the subsiding of these events, the campaign of Armageddon and the tribulation will end. It is fitting that such worldwide catastrophes accompany the global judgment and Christ's second coming.

8. Is there any relationship between the "200 million" of Revelation 9:16 and Armageddon?

Many people have the mistaken idea that the conflict of Armageddon will entail battle with an army of the Antichrist consisting of 200 million troops. It is further held that this army will probably be Chinese. The "200 million" is derived from Revelation 9:16. The Chinese army idea is based on a reported claim by China that it can field such an army, coupled with the "kings of the east" in Revelation 16:12. However, a careful reading of the texts in question shows that the army of 200 million is demonic rather than human and that the events are two separate events. The force of 200 million is *not* part of Armageddon and is *not* Chinese or any other nationality.

The "200 million" is found in the midst of the description of the sixth trumpet judgment of Revelation 9:13-21. This judgment occurs just prior to the middle of the tribulation, three-and-a-half years *before* the conflict of Armageddon, which occurs during the sixth and seventh *bowl* judgments (Revelation 16). Attempts to put the two events together confuses the judgments and chronology of Revelation and the tribulation.

The 200 million are better understood to be demonic because they are led by four fallen angels (Revelation 9:14,15). Revelation 9:17 also describes this army as something other than human: "And this is how I saw in the vision the horses and those who sat on them: the riders had breastplates the color of fire and of hyacinth and of brimstone; and the heads of the horses are like the heads of lions; and out of their mouths proceed fire and smoke and brimstone." If we look at Joel 1:15–2:11 in conjunction with Revelation 9:13-21, we are given a very descriptive image of the sixth trumpet judgment. This army comes from the "bottomless pit," not from a human source. (See Revelation 9:2.) Additionally, "east" in the Bible always refers to Mesopotamia (today: eastern Syria and northern Iraq, between the Tigris and Euphrates Rivers) and, therefore, when they arise in preparation for Armageddon, the "kings of the east" will come from that region rather than China or elsewhere.[14]

It is unfortunate that there has been so much popularization of the "200 million Chinese theory." Such popularization focuses on

Tribulation Judgments from Revelation

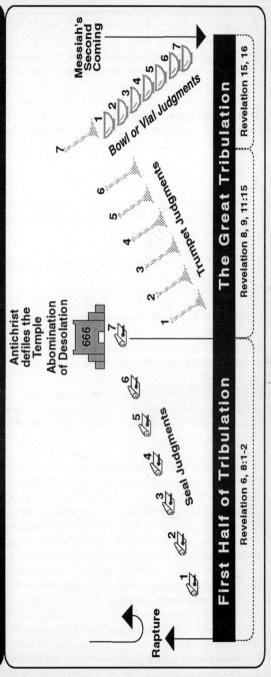

Rapture

First Half of Tribulation
Revelation 6, 8:1-2

Seal Judgments

1 2 3 4 5 6

Antichrist
defiles the
Temple
Abomination
of Desolation

666

7

The Great Tribulation
Revelation 8, 9, 11:15   Revelation 15, 16

Trumpet Judgments

1 2 3 4 5 6

Bowl or Vial Judgments

7 1 2 3 4 5 6 7

Messiah's
Second
Coming

the sensational rather than the sincere and can detract from profitable study of prophecy and the Bible. Dr. Fruchtenbaum writes:

> Sensationalism has had a field day with this figure, resulting in some fantastic speculation. In order for this speculation to stand, the 200 million figure must be pulled out of its context. The speculation all rests on current events. Communist China once declared that they can field an army of 200 million. Without even so much as questioning the truthfulness of this assertion, many have concluded that the 200 million must involve a Chinese invasion of the Middle East. The context just will not allow for this.[15]

Without doubt, Armageddon will involve large armies and vast amounts of military resources. Those resources are not, however, the same as found in Revelation 9.

9. What are the circumstances leading up to Armageddon?

As with many human events, there are two purposes for Armageddon: a divine intent and a human rationale. The divine purpose for Armageddon is judgment in preparation for the 1,000-year reign of Christ on earth. The satan-inspired human purpose is to once-and-for-all eliminate the Jews.

The Divine Purpose

All history and future events are ultimately the outworking of the decree of the Triune God. Nothing takes place that He did not actively plan. Throughout history, the battle has raged between God and Satan, good and evil, although usually not realized by humanity. The war of Armageddon is the culmination of a series of events that climax in this final act. Dr. Paul Feinberg explains:

> Almost every passage that gives us the biblical story shows this supernatural factor at work. In Revelation 16:12-16, the New Testament passage in which we see the word "Armageddon," John sees three evil spirits that look like frogs come out of the mouth of the dragon. These evil spirits went out to the kings of the whole earth to bring them to Armageddon. Great deceptive power was given to these demon spirits so that they could perform miraculous signs. In Zechariah, it is God who says that He will make Jerusalem a burden to all the nations of the world (12:3), and that it is He who will gather all the nations to this city (14:2). . . . The nations have hated God and His people Israel. Now the nations are brought supernaturally to the valley of

Jehoshaphat so that God can enter into judgment against the nations (Joel 3:1-3).[16]

The divine purpose for Armageddon is that it will serve as a venue by which God will judge His enemies. Since both satanic and human opposition is focused on God's elect nation of Israel, they are brought to that location so that God may bring down their foolish schemes of rebellion. The psalmist records God's response of laughter at the puny human plans to overthrow Him at Armageddon:

> Why are the nations in an uproar, and the peoples devising a vain thing? The kings of the earth take their stand, and the rulers take counsel together against the LORD and against His Anointed: "Let us tear their fetters apart, and cast away their cords from us!" He who sits in the heavens laughs, the Lord scoffs at them. Then He will speak to them in His anger and terrify them in His fury: "But as for Me, I have installed My King upon Zion, My holy mountain" (Psalm 2:1-6).

The Human Purpose

The demented human perspective leading to the final march to Jerusalem appears to be motivated by efforts to solve what the majority of the population believes to be the source of the world's problems—the Jews. As we follow the buildup to Armageddon in Revelation (11–18), the persecution of Israel begins at the midpoint of the tribulation and culminates in the worldwide gathering of armies in Israel.

10. What military forces or nations will be involved in Armageddon?

Scripture indicates that all the nations of the world will be gathered in their war against Israel. This is a fitting climax to the tribulation, which evidences the whole world in rebellion against heaven (except for a remnant of believers). Dr. Feinberg explains:

> Not only will this war involve the whole land of Israel, but the Bible teaches that all the nations of the world will also become embroiled in it (Zechariah 12:3; 14:2; Revelation 16:14). These nations quite clearly will form four power blocks or alliances: nations to the south of the land of Palestine; a confederacy from the West; armies from the East (Revelation 16:12); . . . and finally, nations from the north of the land of Israel (Ezekiel 38, 39; Daniel 11:40-45).

When the Bible speaks of all the nations of the whole world, does this mean that every country in existence today will do battle in Armageddon? Obviously not. Just within the last decade, we have seen some nations come and go. None of us can say for sure just what nations will be in existence at the time this prophecy is fulfilled. Will the nations of the Western Hemisphere—the U.S., Canada, and Mexico—be a part of this final conflict? They are not mentioned by name anywhere in the Bible. This does not mean that they will not be in existence, but neither would any prophecy be falsified by their absence.[17]

Scripture emphasizes the kings of the east who take a prominent role in the military buildup in preparation for the war of Armageddon. "And the sixth angel poured out his bowl upon the great river, the Euphrates; and its water was dried up, that the way might be prepared for the kings from the east" (Revelation 16:12). One reason why there is an emphasis on the eastern powers could be because this is where the largest masses of population reside. Not only does this include Middle Eastern nations such as Iran, Iraq, and Saudi Arabia, but even more remote nations such as India, China, Japan, Korea, and so on. Dr. Feinberg tells us:

> Other nations named specifically as participants in this conflict include: Ammon (Jeremiah 9:26; Ezekiel 25:1-7; Daniel 11:41); Assyria (Isaiah 14:24-27); Egypt (Isaiah 19, 20; Ezekiel 29, 30; Daniel 11:41); Libya (Daniel 11:43); Moab (Isaiah 15, 16); and Syria (Isaiah 17), to name just a few. There is also the possibility that Babylon (Isaiah 13, 14, 21) will be rebuilt. Ancient Babylon is modern Iraq and part of Iran. The Bible speaks of its absolute destruction, and this seems never to have occurred historically. While we do not know exactly what nations will be in existence at the time of Armageddon, the Bible states clearly that all those nations which do survive until eschatological times will participate in the meeting at Megiddo.[18]

11. Is Armageddon the only military conflict during the tribulation?

When we consider the fact that, in essence, the whole tribulation will be a war between God and His opponents—Satan, the fallen angels, and mankind—it should not be surprising that there will be a great number of military conflicts throughout. We believe that the tribulation will be a time of great military conflict—so much so that it would not be incorrect to see the tribulation period characterized as a world war.

There are some wars and battles that are specifically mentioned in the Bible in addition to Armageddon. Some of the military conflicts include the Battle of Gog and Magog (Ezekiel

38–39); Jerusalem being surrounded by armies at the midpoint of the tribulation (Daniel 9:27; Matthew 24:15-23); various battles involving the Antichrist's consolidation of global power (Daniel 8:23-27); a battle between the Antichrist and the king of the South (Daniel 11:40-45); and a battle of the armies of the Antichrist at Bozrah (Jeremiah 49:13,14; Micah 2:12). In such a general climate characterized by military conflict, it is not hard to imagine that there will be other battles not specifically mentioned in the Bible. As Matthew 24:6 says, this will be a time of "wars and rumors of wars."

12. What impact will the conflict of Armageddon have on Christians?

After the rapture of the church and the beginning of the tribulation there will many individuals who will come to faith in Jesus Christ. Throughout the seven-year tribulation many of these same Christians will be persecuted and martyred for their faith and for their resistance to the Antichrist. Among these will be those who refuse to take the mark of the beast described in Revelation 13:16-18. Some Christians will probably die in the conflict of Armageddon also.

Though Armageddon will be a time of great death, destruction, and devastation, it will also be a sign to Christians that the end of the tribulation is near. It is for this reason that we find the comforting parenthetical statement by Jesus in verse 15 of the discussion of Armageddon in Revelation 16:12–16:

> Behold, I am coming like a thief. Blessed is the one who stays awake and keeps his garments, lest he walk about naked and men see his shame.

The imagery here is that of taking the clothes of the guard caught sleeping on duty, leaving him naked and disgraced. Jesus is saying believers are not to be like this. Rather, they are to understand the signs and the times. This is the same teaching found in Matthew 24:32-51 and Luke 21:5-36. Christians are encouraged to continue in their faith and to hold on physically and spiritually for a short time longer, for when the armies begin to gather, the return of the Lord and the end is near.

13. What impact will the conflict of Armageddon have on Jerusalem?

Jerusalem will experience both war and peace during the tribulation. It has always been a city whose daily life swings as a pendulum between these two conditions. In the tribulation, the pendulum will swing even faster. In the first half of the tribulation there will peace in the city, although other disasters will befall it from the seal and trumpet judgments of Revelation 6, 8, and 9.

At some point during the tribulation, Israel will experience the fighting and events of Ezekiel 38–39, where armies from Gog and Magog will come against the nation. These forces will be destroyed by God through natural disasters and internal dissension (Ezekiel 38:17-23).

In the second half of the tribulation the city will experience war and fighting, especially at the end when the battle of Armageddon ensues. According to Zechariah 14:1-3, armies will be fighting in Jerusalem on the very day of the second coming of Christ:

> Behold, a day is coming for the LORD when the spoil taken from you will be divided among you. For I will gather all the nations against Jerusalem to battle, and the city will be captured, the houses plundered, the women ravished, and half of the city exiled, but the rest of the people will not be cut off from the city. Then the LORD will go forth and fight against those nations, as when He fights on a day of battle.

Under attack, Jerusalem will receive supernatural strength and the city will be victorious:

> In that day the LORD will defend the inhabitants of Jerusalem, and the one who is feeble among them in that day will be like David, and the house of David will be like God, like the angel of the LORD before them. And it will come about in that day that I will set about to destroy all the nations that come against Jerusalem (Zechariah 12:8,9).

Whether one believes that Armageddon will be a single battle or a campaign that encompasses days or even years, the battle will affect Jerusalem. Ultimately the security of the city will be assured only by the return of Christ—but not before the city is attacked and many people flee. Future victory in Jerusalem is certain . . . but so is combat.

14. What impact will the conflict of Armageddon have on Babylon?

In the course of developments relating to Armageddon, Babylon* will be destroyed. Revelation 16 indicates that the final two bowl

---

* See Question 1 for a description of Babylon.

judgments are related to Babylon and Armageddon. The sixth bowl judgment is poured out "upon the great river, the Euphrates; and its water was dried up, that the way might be prepared for the kings from the east" (verse 12) that they may be gathered "together to the place which in Hebrew is called Har-Magedon" (verse 16). In conjunction with the sixth, the seventh bowl judgment follows with the judgment of Babylon (Revelation 16:17-21). Revelation 16:19 describes this judgment: "And the great city was split into three parts, and the cities of the nations fell. And Babylon the great was remembered before God, to give her the cup of the wine of His fierce wrath."

Babylon, God's ancient enemy, will meet her Waterloo in conjunction with the war of Armageddon. Destroyed in one hour and gone forever will be political, religious, and commercial Babylon. Frankly, for believers, it should be a day we look forward to. Finally God will make right the wrongs of Babylon:

> For this reason in one day her plagues will come, pestilence and mourning and famine, and she will be burned up with fire; for the Lord God who judges her is strong. And the kings of the earth, who committed acts of immorality and lived sensuously with her, will weep and lament over her when they see the smoke of her burning, standing at a distance because of the fear of her torment, saying, "Woe, woe, the great city, Babylon, the strong city! For in one hour your judgment has come" (Revelation 18:8-10).

P A R T   3

What Else Do We Know About Armageddon?

15. How does Armageddon relate to Israel's conversion?

Armageddon relates significantly to Israel's conversion and, in a very real way, is a major cause for her conversion. Scripture teaches that when Jerusalem is surrounded by the armies of the Antichrist and the world, who are poised to destroy Israel, the wayward nation will recognize that Jesus of Nazareth is truly their long-awaited Messiah. Notice what the Lord said through His prophet Zechariah:

> "Behold, I am going to make Jerusalem a cup that causes reeling to all the peoples around; and when the siege is against Jerusalem, it will also be against Judah. And it will come about in that day that I will make Jerusalem a heavy

stone for all the peoples; all who lift it will be severely injured. And all the nations of the earth will be gathered against it.

"In that day," declares the LORD, "I will strike every horse with bewilderment, and his rider with madness. But I will watch over the house of Judah, while I strike every horse of the peoples with blindness. Then the clans of Judah will say in their hearts, 'A strong support for us are the inhabitants of Jerusalem through the LORD of hosts, their God.' In that day I will make the clans of Judah like a firepot among pieces of wood and a flaming torch among sheaves, so they will consume on the right hand and on the left all the surrounding peoples, while the inhabitants of Jerusalem again dwell on their own sites in Jerusalem.

"The LORD also will save the tents of Judah first in order that the glory of the house of David and the glory of the inhabitants of Jerusalem may not be magnified above Judah. In that day the LORD will defend the inhabitants of Jerusalem, and the one who is feeble among them in that day will be like David, and the house of David will be like God, like the angel of the LORD before them. And it will come about in that day that I will set about to destroy all the nations that come against Jerusalem. And I will pour out on the house of David and on the inhabitants of Jerusalem, the Spirit of grace and of supplication, so that they will look on Me whom they have pierced; and they will mourn for Him, as one mourns for an only son, and they will weep bitterly over Him, like the bitter weeping over a first-born.

"In that day there will be great mourning in Jerusalem, like the mourning of Hadadrimmon in the plain of Megiddo. And the land will mourn, every family by itself; the family of the house of David by itself, and their wives by themselves; the family of the house of Nathan by itself, and their wives by themselves; the family of the house of Levi by itself, and their wives by themselves; the family of the Shimeites by itself, and their wives by themselves; all the families that remain, every family by itself, and their wives by themselves. In that day a fountain will be opened for the house of David and for the inhabitants of Jerusalem, for sin and for impurity" (Zechariah 12:2–13:1).

It is clear that Armageddon is the historical context in which Israel is converted. It is Israel's conversion that leads the Jews to call upon their newly found Messiah for the second coming (Matthew

23:39) so they may be physically rescued from the Antichrist's efforts to exterminate their race (Romans 10:13,14).

16. How does the Antichrist relate to Armageddon?

The Antichrist is soundly in the middle of the Battle of Armageddon. He is the primary human involved in conceiving, planning, and executing the campaign.

After Babylon is destroyed (Revelation 16–18), the Antichrist is furious at the Lord of Heaven. With revenge in his heart he turns his fury toward Israel and God's people, the Jews (Daniel 11:38,39). As he waits in Israel for all his armies to arrive (Daniel 11:45) for his attack upon Jerusalem, his anger is likely building against God and His people. His wrath has directed him exactly where God intends him to be. Now our Lord is ready for the action to begin, as recorded in Joel:

> Proclaim this among the nations: prepare a war; rouse the mighty men! Let all the soldiers draw near, let them come up! Beat your plowshares into swords, and your pruning hooks into spears; let the weak say, "I am a mighty man." Hasten and come, all you surrounding nations, and gather yourselves there. Bring down, O LORD, Thy mighty ones. Let the nations be aroused and come up to the valley of Jehoshaphat, for there I will sit to judge all the surrounding nations. Put in the sickle, for the harvest is ripe. Come, tread, for the wine press is full; the vats overflow, for their wickedness is great. Multitudes, multitudes in the valley of decision! For the day of the LORD is near in the valley of decision. The sun and moon grow dark, and the stars lose their brightness. And the LORD roars from Zion and utters His voice from Jerusalem, and the heavens and the earth tremble. But the LORD is a refuge for His people and a stronghold to the sons of Israel. Then you will know that I am the LORD your God, dwelling in Zion My holy mountain. So Jerusalem will be holy, and strangers will pass through it no more (3:9-17).

It will be on this day in history, during the battle of Armageddon, that the Antichrist will be captured by Jesus Christ and His human and angelic army. The beast (as the book of Revelation refers to the Antichrist) is taken and thrown forever into the lake of fire.

> And I saw an angel standing in the sun; and he cried out with a loud voice, saying to all the birds which fly in midheaven,

"Come, assemble for the great supper of God; in order that you may eat the flesh of kings and the flesh of commanders and the flesh of mighty men and the flesh of horses and of those who sit on them and the flesh of all men, both free men and slaves, and small and great."

And I saw the beast and the kings of the earth and their armies, assembled to make war against Him who sat upon the horse, and against His army. And the beast was seized, and with him the false prophet who performed the signs in his presence, by which he deceived those who had received the mark of the beast and those who worshiped his image; these two were thrown alive into the lake of fire which burns with brimstone. And the rest were killed with the sword which came from the mouth of Him who sat upon the horse, and all the birds were filled with their flesh (Revelation 19:17-21)

At the end of Armageddon, the Antichrist's day of victory will be turned into everlasting defeat.

17. How does Jesus Christ relate to Armageddon?

Christ is the star of the Armageddon show. Jesus Christ stands the satanic intent of crushing Israel at Armageddon on its head by returning to rescue His newly converted people. Revelation 19:11-16 describes Christ's grand return to the stage of earth history. At Armageddon the hero is not hard to spot because he shows up riding a white horse:

And I saw heaven opened; and behold, a white horse, and He who sat upon it is called Faithful and True; and in righteousness He judges and wages war. And His eyes are a flame of fire, and upon His head are many diadems; and He has a name written upon Him which no one knows except Himself. And He is clothed with a robe dipped in blood; and His name is called The Word of God. And the armies which are in heaven, clothed in fine linen, white and clean, were following Him on white horses. And from His mouth comes a sharp sword, so that with it He may smite the nations; and He will rule them with a rod of iron; and He treads the wine press of the fierce wrath of God, the Almighty. And on His robe and on His thigh He has a name written, "KING OF KINGS, AND LORD OF LORDS."

In the early 1970s there was a cartoon in a Christian publication that depicted Armageddon. The drawing included a five-star general standing on a hill overlooking a military battle taking place in the valley below. This was clearly Armageddon. Looking through his binoculars, the general's attention was focused on the battle below. The general's assistant was simultaneously nudging his commander and looking up and pointing at the sky. In the sky was a classic depiction of Christ's return on a white horse with His heavenly armies following. The caption had the assistant telling the general something like, "Sir! I think the direction of the battle is about to change!" What an understatement! Christ's role in Armageddon will be to not only turn the battle against the Antichrist, but also transition history from the horrors of the tribulation to the blessings of the millennial kingdom.

At Armageddon, Christ will disrupt the flow of events by returning in judgment in preparation for His glorious 1,000-year reign upon planet Earth. Like a child awaking from a nightmare to find that he is really safe, so will be the rescue of God's people Israel (Matthew 24:29-31). The turmoil of Armageddon and the Middle East becomes a long-awaited peace. Christ finally brings the long prophesied "shalom" of the Bible to rule in the hearts of His people, and, at this time, to rule in the human affairs of His people. He brings the world to a new beginning.

18. Where does the Bible teach that Jesus will return to the Mount of Olives?

In the first chapter of Acts we read of the ascent of Jesus from the Mount of Olives after the resurrection and the 40 days with the disciples. As the disciples stood watching the ascent, two angels appeared to them telling them that Jesus would return to the same location: "Men of Galilee, why do you stand looking into the sky? This Jesus, who has been taken up from you into heaven, will come in just the same way as you have watched Him go into heaven" (Acts 1:11). Jesus' first-century departure was prefigured in the sixth century B.C. when Ezekiel watched the glory of God depart from Israel's temple and descend from the Mount of Olives.

The return of Christ, or the second coming (not the rapture), was prophesied by Zechariah almost six hundred years earlier in Zechariah 14:4: "And in that day His feet will stand on the Mount of Olives, which is in front of Jerusalem on the east; and the Mount of Olives will be split in its middle from east to west by a very large valley, so that half of the mountain will move toward the north and the other half toward the south." Since Christ delivered His great prophetic discourse on His second coming from the Mount of Olives, it is clearly implied that His return will be at the same location (Matthew 24–25). This will be Christ's victory ascent after defeating the Antichrist and his forces. (This coming should not be confused with the rapture, which occurs seven years earlier and is recorded in 1 Thessalonians 4:14-17. These two comings are separate and distinct events.)[19]

19. What happens after Armageddon?

Armageddon culminates in the second coming of Jesus Christ to the earth and the destruction of the forces of the Antichrist. This will conclude the 7-year tribulation. There will then be a 75-day transition period between the tribulation and the 1,000-year reign of Jesus Christ upon the earth known as the millennium (see Question 20).[20] In this interim period, the image of the Antichrist that was set up in the temple at the middle of the tribulation will be removed after 30 days (Daniel 12:11). According to Revelation 19:20, the Antichrist and the False Prophet will be cast into the lake of fire at this point. Since the Antichrist was killed at the second coming of Christ, he will be resurrected for this punishment. Satan will also be bound at this time for the duration of the millennium (Revelation 20:1-3). During this time, Jewish survivors of the tribulation will be judged (Ezekiel 20:34-38), as well as living Gentiles and the nations who persecuted the Jews during the tribulation (Joel 3:1-3; Matthew 25:31-46). This will also be the time of the resurrection of Old Testament saints (Isaiah 26:19; Daniel 12:2) and the resurrection of tribulation saints (Revelation 20:4-6).

Following this interval will be the millennial kingdom of Jesus Christ as foretold in passages such as Isaiah 2:2-4; Ezekiel 37:1-13; 40–48; Micah 4:1-7; and Revelation 20.[21] In Psalm 2:6-9, the psalmist tells of the yet future reign of Jesus Christ:

> "But as for Me, I have installed My King Upon Zion, My holy mountain. I will surely tell of the decree of the LORD: He said to Me, 'Thou art My Son, today I have begotten Thee. Ask of Me, and I will surely give the nations as Thine inheritance, and the very ends of the earth as Thy possession. Thou shalt break them with a rod of iron, Thou shalt shatter them like earthenware.' "

An earthly kingdom with a physical presence and rule by the Messiah-King is foretold throughout the Bible. This promise was not fulfilled in the first coming of Jesus Christ (when He did what only He could do—die on the cross to pay for sin) because, though offered, the kingdom was rejected by Israel and, thus, it was postponed until the second coming of Christ. Revelation 5 says that Christ is worthy to receive this kingdom, and in Revelation 11:15 we are told that the prophecies will yet be fulfilled. The millennium is a transitional period in God's program; it is the beginning of the eternal rule of God in the kingdom, which will pass into the eternal state. It is "the consummating link between history and the eternal order."[22] History and current events are moving toward a final era that will be the pinnacle of God's plan. Dr. David Larsen, citing the French theologian René Pache, writes:

> If history culminated with cataclysm and judgment, the Second Coming of Christ in power would be only "a walk through the ruins." The stone which becomes a mountain will "fill all the earth" (Daniel 2:35). "They will reign on earth" is the promise (Revelation 5:10). The venue of the Kingdom is to be on earth before we come to the final expression of the Kingdom in "the new heaven and the new earth" (2 Peter 3:13; Revelation 21–22).[23]

The millennium will be followed by the final judgment and the eternal state. At this point, Armageddon will be an event 1,000 years old, and the horrors of it will be replaced by the joys of eternal worship and eternal life.

20. Why is there a 75-day interval between Jesus' second coming and the millennium?

Careful reading of the Bible reveals that there is an interval of 75 days between the tribulation and the millennium. This interval comes at the end of the tribulation, after the second coming of Jesus Christ and the end of the Armageddon conflict. According to Daniel 12:11,12 mention is made of 1,290 days from the midpoint of the tribulation:

> And from the time that the regular sacrifice is abolished, and the abomination of desolation is set up, there will be 1,290 days. How blessed is he who keeps waiting and attains to the 1,335 days!

An extra 30 days are added to the normal three and a half years (1,260 days) giving a total of 1,290 days. Note that Daniel then says, "How blessed is he who keeps waiting and attains to the 1,335 days." The extra 30 days added to the 45 days (1,335 − 45 = 1,290) comes to a total of 75 days. This will likely be the time in which the sheep and goat judgment of Matthew 25:31-46 takes place. This also might be additional time for setting up the millennium after the devastation of the tribulation.

21. Do the events of Ezekiel 38–39 relate to Armageddon?

The two chapters of Ezekiel 38–39 prophesy a great campaign and battle in the Middle East, but there is not unanimous agreement by prophecy scholars on when it occurs. Within premillennialism there are at least six views on the timing of the events in these chapters. Each view has some strengths and objections to it.[24] The views regarding the timing of these chapters are as follows:

1. Before the tribulation begins (but not necessarily before the rapture)
2. At the midpoint of the tribulation
3. At the end of the tribulation and as part of Armageddon
4. Throughout the second half of the tribulation (chapter 38 at the midpoint and chapter 39 at the end)
5. After the tribulation but prior to the millennium
6. At the end of the millennium

There are several details of these chapters that differ from accounts of Armageddon in Revelation that lead us away from strict identification of it with Armageddon. Fruchtenbaum summarizes these:

> First, in Ezekiel there are definite allies mentioned and they are limited in number while other nations stand in opposition. In the Campaign of Armageddon all nations are allied together against Jerusalem without exception. Secondly, the Ezekiel invasion comes from the north, but the Armageddon invasion comes from the whole earth. Thirdly, the purpose of the Russian [38:6] invasion is to take spoil; the purpose of the Armageddon Campaign is to destroy all the Jews. Fourthly, in the Ezekiel invasion there is a protest against the invasion; in the Armageddon Campaign there is no protest since all the nations are involved. Fifthly, the Ezekiel invasion is destroyed through convulsions of nature; the Armageddon invasion is destroyed by the personal second coming of Jesus Christ. Sixthly, the Ezekiel invasion is destroyed on the mountains of Israel; the Armageddon Campaign is destroyed in the area between Petra and Jerusalem. Seventh, the Russian invasion takes place while Israel is living securely in the land; but the Armageddon Campaign takes place while Israel is in flight and in hiding.[25]

Two of the major issues that any view must address is that of the seven months to bury the dead from the battle (Ezekiel 39:12-14) and the seven years of burning the weapons (Ezekiel 39:9,10). In the second half of the tribulation the Jews are fleeing and being persecuted; therefore, the burying of the dead is a problem. Also, of the six major views, only the first one doesn't place some of the burning of the weapons beyond the seven-year tribulation and into the millennium. (In the case of the sixth view, into the eternal state, which makes no sense.) For some, the issue of weapons in the millennium is not an issue but is seen as fitting with other statements such as beating swords into plowshares and spears into pruning hooks (Isaiah 2:4; Micah 4:3).[26]

Proponents of each view are trying to put the pieces of this portion of the prophetic puzzle together. To do so, there must be consistent interpretation of the various texts and proper identification of all the various elements in the chapters. Though not necessarily controversial, the chapters are detailed, and there has been much legitimate speculation about the details. Many interpreters opt to place these chapters at the end of the tribulation (and associate them with Armageddon) or beginning at the middle of the tribulation and carrying through to the end. However, Dr. Fruchtenbaum holds the view that the events are prior to the tribulation but not necessarily prior to the rapture. Such a view allows the possibility (though not necessity) of a significant lapse between the rapture and the beginning of the tribulation, which comes with the signing of the seven-year covenant (Daniel 9:27). There are several strong points to be made in support of this view. First, the nation of Israel today is populated by Jews and other peoples from many nations (Ezekiel 38:8,12). Second, the Jews dwell securely (Ezekiel 38:11,14), even though not always peacefully. Third, this view allows for the seven years and seven months with no difficulty.[27] While some have tried to argue that such a view destroys the doctrine of imminency in relation to the rapture, such is not the case, for, as he points out, "stating that something must precede the tribulation is *not* the same as stating that it must precede the rapture unless it is further stated that the rapture begins the tribulation. However, the act that begins the tribulation is not the rapture but the signing of the seven year covenant."[28]

Whichever view one holds, there is the certainty that these chapters will yet be fulfilled and that at least one and very likely two great military campaigns will occur in the Middle East in the coming years. It doesn't appear that the events of Ezekiel 38–39 relate to Armageddon.

22. Why must Armageddon occur?

From a human perspective, Armageddon will be a horrible war of mass destruction. It will be the culmination of the greatest time of terror the world has known. Wouldn't it be better for all of this not to happen? Dr. Charles Ryrie writes:

> Why must there be such a time as this? There are at least two reasons: First, the wickedness of man must be punished. God may seem to be doing nothing about evil now, but someday He will act. A second reason is that man must, by one means

or another, be prostrated before the King of kings and Lord of lords. He may do so voluntarily now by coming to Christ in faith and receiving salvation. Later he will *have* to do so, receiving only condemnation.[29]

23. How do current events in the Middle East relate to Armageddon?

Current events in the Middle East do not relate directly to the next prophetic *event* on God's calendar—the rapture of the church. However, they do relate, prophetically, to the next *phase* of history, which is the tribulation. Since the seven-year tribulation will climax in the battle of Armageddon in the Middle East, then events occurring today are preparatory for the tribulation and can be tracked as setting the stage for the future. Dr. John Walvoord explains:

> The world today is like a stage being set for a great drama. The major actors are already in the wings waiting for their moment in history. The main stage props are already in place. The prophetic play is about to begin. . . . All the necessary historical developments have already taken place.[30]

These major situations that are true now, and that were not true fifty years ago, point to the conclusion that the Rapture itself may be very near because the stage has been set for events that will follow the Rapture.

> All areas of prophecy combine in the united testimony that history is preparing our generation for the end of the age.

> In each area of prophecy a chronological checklist of important prophetic events can be compiled. In each list, in regard to the church, the nations, or Israel, the events of history clearly indicate that the world is poised and ready for the Rapture of the church and the beginning of the countdown to Armageddon. [31]

Earlier, Dr. Walvoord notes:

> Never before in history have all the factors been present for the fulfillment of prophecy relating to end-time religious trends and events. Only in our generation have the combined revival of Israel, the formation of a world church, the increasing power of Muslim religion, the rise of the occult, and the worldwide spread of atheistic philosophy been present as a dramatic setting for the final fulfillment of prophecy. As far

as world religion is concerned, the road to Armageddon is already well prepared, and those who will travel to their doom may well be members of our present generation.[32]

P A R T   4

Why Does Armageddon Matter?

---

24. Why should I be concerned about Armageddon?

As a Christian living before the rapture of the church and before the conflict of Armageddon, the perspective is very different from the one that new believers will have after the rapture. We will not experience either the tribulation or the campaign of Armageddon; they may experience both. Yet Armageddon is important for us, not because we are to be "Christian Chicken Littles," who panic and say that the end is near, but because we are to be discerning students of the Bible who realize that God has a plan for the world and history is "going somewhere." God has told us some of the future through biblical prophecy. We do not know the future fully, but we know with certainty that God is presently working in the lives of people and the events of each day. Through past and present events, God is working to set the stage for the final act of world history. It is an act in which Jesus Christ will reign supreme, and Armageddon is one scene in that closing act.

As Christians we should also express concern about Armageddon because of the devastation and death that will occur. The biblical glimpses of the conflict should serve as a catalyst for evangelism, obedience, and prayer—for believers and nonbelievers. For those who do not know Jesus Christ, the future in this world and the next will be tragic. Armageddon serves as a warning of the coming judgment and an encouragement to seek a personal relationship with Jesus Christ—the Messiah and Savior.

25. How should I pray for Jerusalem and the Middle East?

Journalists, diplomats, politicians, and historians frequently use the phrase "peace and prosperity." However, from a biblical perspective, "peace and *salvation*" is correct. We should pray daily for peace in the Middle East so that the gospel and the message of Jesus Christ can spread unimpeded (1 Timothy 2:1-4). Recognizing God's prophetic plan, we should also pray for the salvation of all people who inhabit that region.

The pain, pride, prejudice, and politics of the Middle East is very real. The suffering has been immense and the solutions are elusive. Yet the prophecies are as real as the problems, and the solution rests ultimately in the Scripture and the Savior.

As we await the return of Jesus Christ, Jerusalem's Messiah-King, we should heed the words of King David:

> Pray for the peace of Jerusalem: "May they prosper who love you. May peace be within your walls, and prosperity within your palaces." For the sake of my brothers and my friends, I will now say, "May peace be within you" (Psalm 122:6-9).

26. What is the hope for the future?

The hope for the Christian continues to be the return of the Lord Jesus Christ for His own in the rapture. Titus 2:13 admonishes believers to be "looking for the blessed hope and the appearing of the glory of our great God and Savior, Christ Jesus." In the interim, we are to be faithful to Him, to proclaim the gospel of salvation to all who will listen, and to "do good to all men, and especially those who are of the household of the faith" (Galatians 6:10). Christians are not pessimistic about the future; rather, we are realistic and know that, regardless of tomorrow's headlines, our hope and our destiny is in Christ Jesus, the final victor.

CONCLUSION

Armageddon will be the last great world war of history. It will take place in Israel in conjunction with the second coming of Christ. The Bible is very clear that it is a certain and cataclysmic event yet to come. According to the Bible, great armies from the east and the west will gather and assemble to strike a final blow against Israel. There will be threats to the power of the Antichrist from the south, and he will also move to destroy a revived Babylon in the east before finally turning his forces toward Jerusalem. As he and his armies move on Jerusalem, God will intervene and Jesus Christ will return to rescue His people, Israel. The Lord and His angelic army will destroy the armies, capture the Antichrist and the False Prophet, and cast them into the lake of fire (Revelation 19:11-21).

In a sense, Armageddon is a battle that never really takes place. That is, it does not take place in accordance with its human intent to gather the armies of the world to execute the Antichrist's solution to the "Jewish problem." This is why Jesus Christ chooses this moment in history for His return to earth. He will thwart the Antichrist's attempted annihilation of the Jews and destroy the armies of the world who have been gathered for that purpose. It seems only fitting, in light of mankind's bloody legacy, that the return of Christ should be precipitated by worldwide military conflict against Israel. History is moving toward Armageddon.

Notes

1. Charles H. Dyer, *World News and Bible Prophecy* (Wheaton, IL: Tyndale House Publishers, 1991), pp. 237-38.
2. Arnold G. Fruchtenbaum, *The Footsteps of the Messiah: A Study of the Sequence of Prophetic Events* (Tustin, CA: Ariel Press, 1982), p. 254.
3. Ibid., p. 218.
4. For more details on the rapture, see our *Truth About the Rapture* in this same series.
5. See J. Dwight Pentecost, *Things to Come: A Study in Biblical Eschatology* (Grand Rapids: Zondervan Publishing House, 1958), pp. 346-55.
6. Fruchtenbaum, *Footsteps,* pp. 216-53.
7. Ibid., p. 216.
8. Ibid., p. 217.
9. Ibid., p. 223.
10. Ibid., pp. 201-04.
11. Ibid., p. 233.
12. Ibid., p. 239.
13. Ibid., p. 248.
14. Ibid., p. 217.
15. Ibid., p. 155.
16. Paul Feinberg, "The Mideast March to Megiddo," in William T. James, ed., *Foreshocks of Antichrist* (Eugene, OR: Harvest House Publishers, 1997), pp. 270-71.
17. Ibid., p. 262.
18. Ibid., pp. 263-64.
19. For more information on the rapture, see our *Truth About the Rapture* (Harvest House Publishers, 1996), pp. 26-33.
20. See Fruchtenbaum, *Footsteps,* pp. 256-63, for a full discussion of this interval.
21. For a fuller discussion see our *Truth About the Millennium* in this same series.
22. David Larsen, *Jews, Gentiles, and the Church: A New Perspective on History and Prophecy* (Grand Rapids: Discovery House, 1995), p. 316.
23. Ibid., p. 317.
24. See Fruchtenbaum, *Footsteps,* pp. 77-83; and Harold W. Hoehner, "The Progression of Events in Ezekiel 38–39" in Charles H. Dyer and Roy B. Zuck, *Integrity of Heart, Skillfulness of Hands* (Grand Rapids: Baker Books, 1994), pp. 82-92.
25. Fruchtenbaum, *Footsteps,* pp. 78-79.
26. Harold W. Hoehner, "The Progression of Events in Ezekiel 38–39," in Charles H. Dyer and Roy B. Zuck, *Intergrity of Heart, Skillfulness of Hands* (Grand Rapids: Baker Books, 1994).
27. Fruchtenbaum holds that the invasion "must take place at least 3 fi years or more before the tribulation starts" (*Footsteps,* p. 81), so that the 7 years would be completed by the middle of the tribulation, though not all who hold this view require such a large time period.
28. Fruchtenbaum, *Footsteps,* p. 82.

29. Charles C. Ryrie, *Basic Theology* (Wheaton, IL: Victory Books, 1986), p. 476.

30. John F. Walvoord, *Armageddon, Oil and the Middle East Crisis* (Grand Rapids: Zondervan Publishing House, 1990), p. 227.

31. Ibid., p. 219. See also our *Truth About the Signs of the Times* in this Pocket Prophecy series.

32. Walvoord, *Armageddon*, p. 120.

Recommended Reading

Chambers, Joseph. *A Palace for the Antichrist: Saddam Hussein's Drive to Rebuild Babylon and Its Place in Bible Prophecy.* Green Forest, AR: New Leaf Press, 1996.

Dyer, Charles H. *The Rise of Babylon: Sign of the End Times.* Wheaton, IL: Tyndale House Publishers, 1991.

_____. *World News and Bible Prophecy.* Wheaton, IL: Tyndale House Publishers, 1993.

_____. "The Identity of Babylon in Revelation 17–18, parts 1 and 2." *Bibliotheca Sacra* (vol. 145; nos. 575, 576), pp. 305-16, 433-49.

Feinberg, Charles L. *The Prophecy of Ezekiel: The Glory of the Lord.* Chicago: Moody Press, 1969.

Feinberg, Paul. "The Mideast March to Megiddo," in William T. James, ed., *Foreshocks of Antichrist.* Eugene, OR: Harvest House Publishers, 1997, pp. 255-73.

Fruchtenbaum, Arnold. *The Footsteps of the Messiah: A Study of the Sequence of Prophetic Events.* San Antonio, TX: Ariel press, 1982.

Hoehner, Harold W. "The Progression of Events in Ezekiel 38–39" in *Integrity of Heart, Skillfulness of Hands: Biblical and Leadership Studies in Honor of Donald K. Campbell,* Charles H. Dyer and Roy B. Zuck eds. Grand Rapids: Baker Books, 1994, pp. 82-91.

Ice, Thomas and Demy, Timothy. *The Truth About 2000 A.D. and Predicting Christ's Return.* Eugene, OR: Harvest House Publishers, 1996.

_____. *The Truth About the Antichrist and His Kingdom.* Eugene, OR: Harvest House Publishers, 1996.

_____. *The Truth About Jerusalem in Bible Prophecy.* Eugene, OR: Harvest House Publishers, 1996.

_____. *The Truth About the Millennium.* Eugene, OR: Harvest House Publishers, 1996.

_____. *The Truth About the Signs of the Times.* Eugene, OR: Harvest House Publishers, 1997.

_____. *The Truth About the Tribulation.* Eugene, OR: Harvest House Publishers, 1996.

James, Edgar. *Arabs, Oil, and Armageddon.* Chicago: Moody Press, 1991.

James, William T. *Storming Toward Armageddon: Essays in Apocalypse.* Green Forest, AR: New Leaf Press, 1992.

Jeffrey, Grant R. *Armageddon: Appointment with Destiny.* Toronto: Frontier Research Publications, 1988.

Lindsey, Hal. *The Final Battle.* Palos Verdes, CA: Western Front, Ltd., 1995.

Lindsey, Hal, with C.C. Carlson. *The Late Great Planet Earth.* Grand Rapids: Zondervan Publishing House, 1970.

Pentecost, J. Dwight. *Things to Come: A Study in Biblical Eschatology.* Grand Rapids: Zondervan Publishing House, 1958.

Rosen, Moishe. *Beyond the Gulf War: Overture to Armageddon?* San Bernardino, CA: Here's Life Publishers, 1991.

Ryrie, Charles C. *Basic Theology.* Wheaton, IL: SP Publications, 1987.

Thomas, Robert L. *Revelation: An Exegetical Commentary.* 2 vols. Chicago: Moody Press, 1995.

Walvoord, John F. *Armageddon, Oil and the Middle East Crisis.* Rev. ed. Grand Rapids: Zondervan Publishing House, 1990.

_____. *Daniel: The Key to Prophetic Revelation.* Chicago: Moody Press, 1971.

_____. *Israel in Prophecy.* Grand Rapids: Zondervan Publishing House, 1962.

_____. *Major Bible Prophecies: 37 Crucial Prophecies That Affect You Today.* Grand Rapids: Zondervan Publishing House, 1991.

_____. *The Nations in Prophecy.* Grand Rapids: Zondervan Publishing House, 1967.

_____. *Prophecy: 14 Essential Keys to Understanding the Final Drama.* Nashville: Thomas Nelson Publishers, 1993.

_____. *The Prophecy Knowledge Handbook.* Wheaton, IL: SP Publications, 1990.

_____. *The Revelation of Jesus Christ.* Chicago: Moody Press, 1963.

Yamauchi, Edwin. *Foes from the Northern Frontier.* Grand Rapids: Baker Books, 1982.

_____. "Russian Attacks?" *Biblical Archeologist,* Spring 1983: 96-97.

_____. "The Scythians: Invading Hordes from the Russian Steppes" *Biblical Archeologist,* Spring 1983: 90-95, 98-99.

For additional information contact:

Pre-Trib Research Center
10400 Courthouse Rd., Suite 241
Spotsylvania, VA 22553